Cross Stitch

A beginner's step-by-step guide to techniques and motifs

CHARLOTTE GERLINGS

FOX CHAPEL
PUBLISHING

To Thelma M. Nye, craft editor at B. T. Batsford Ltd. for over thirty years, and friend and advisor to many grateful authors and designers.

Front cover: buttons produced and photographed by Sam Gillespie
Back cover: photographs reproduced by kine permission of Madeira UK and DMC Creative World Ltd.

First published in the United Kingdom by Arcturus Publishing Limited, 2011.
First published in North America in 2012, revised, by Fox Chapel Publishing, 1970 Broad Street, East Petersburg, PA 17520.

ISBN 978-1-56523-684-4

Front cover buttons produced and photographed by Sam Gillespie.
Back cover materials provided and photographed by DMC Creative World Ltd. (www.dmccreative.co.uk) and Madeira UK (www.madeira.co.uk).

Illustrated by David Woodroffe

Library of Congress Cataloging-in-Publication Data

Gerlings, Charlotte.
 Cross stitch / Charlotte Gerlings.
   p. cm. -- (Craft wookbooks)
 ISBN 978-1-56523-684-4
 1. Cross-stitch--Patterns. I. Title.
 TT778.C76G42 2011
 746.44'3--dc23
                  2011024128

Fox Chapel Publishing, or to find a retailer near you, call toll-free 800-457-9112 or visit us at *www.FoxChapelPublishing.com*.

Note to Authors: We are always looking for talented authors to write new books. Please send a brief letter describing your idea to Acquisition Editor, 1970 Broad Street, East Petersburg, PA 17520.

Printed in China
First printing

CONTENTS

Introduction 4

PART I: EQUIPMENT AND MATERIALS

Needles and fabrics 5

Equipment 6

Working with hoops and frames 7

Needles 8

Threads 9

Fabrics and thread counts 10

Calculating quantities 11

Cross stitch charts and how to read them 12

Charting your own design 13

Blank cross stitch grids 14

Readymades 16

PART II: CROSS STITCH METHODS AND TECHNIQUES

Thread organizer 17

Preparing fabric 18

Preparing threads 20

Starting and fastening off 21

Basic stitches 22

The history of samplers 24

Backstitch alphabet 25

Popular sampler motifs 26

Assisi work 27

Heraldic beasts and mythical creatures 28

Assisi-style alphabet 29

Cross stitch variations 30

Sans serif alphabet plus numerals 32

Serif alphabet plus numerals 33

Knot stitches 34

PART III: STITCHABLES

Templates 35

Greetings cards 36

Decorative bands 37

Working with plastic canvas 38

Miniature designs 39

Borders and corners 40

PART IV: BASIC EMBROIDERY STITCHES

Basic embroidery stitches 41

Script alphabet 44

Washing, mounting and aftercare 45

Terms and abbreviations 47

INTRODUCTION

Cross stitch is one of the oldest forms of hand embroidery, popular all over the world, and it is little wonder that it remains so. Not only is it easy to learn—cross stitch is usually the first embroidery stitch taught to children —but it's quickly arranged into patterns, pictures and letters by following grid charts where each square represents a single stitch. The pleasure in achievement can become quite addictive as the design grows and different colors are added.

This book has been prepared with beginners in mind. The essentials of counted cross stitch are set out here with plenty of illustrations to guide you, and a basic range of free-style embroidery stitches has been added in a supplement to the counted thread method. The book also aims to act as a refresher for those who first learned to cross stitch years ago and would like to pick it up again. There are sections on equipment and various threads and fabrics, as well as advice on how to read charts and create your own, including numerous motifs and alphabets for you to use. Although this book was originally published in the UK, the technical terms and phrases throughout have been revised with a US audience in mind.

The art of cross stitch dates back at least as far as the 6th or 7th century CE when it was used to decorate household linens with floral or geometric patterns, worked simply in black or red thread. Folk costumes, especially from northern and eastern Europe, are often decorated with similar traditional designs; medieval Assisi work and Tudor blackwork were beautiful, intricate developments of the same technique. Later came the familiar multicolored sampler, which served several purposes: to record patterns or motifs in the absence of pattern books; to teach children how to stitch; and finally to demonstrate a young woman's prowess with the needle.

Today, we happily incorporate cross stitch designs into many items, from greetings cards to buttons, bookmarks, pot covers and paperweights; while larger projects—including elaborate pre-printed kits—are stitched with skill and patience, hopefully to be framed as future family heirlooms.

PART ONE:

EQUIPMENT AND MATERIALS

NEEDLES AND FABRICS

Needles are manufactured in various thicknesses for different uses. The following chart is a general guide to the size of needle suitable for cross stitch on Aida or evenweave fabrics. The higher the number, the finer the needle. Dimensions may vary slightly between manufacturers.

NEEDLE SIZE	FABRIC	NEEDLE LENGTH	EYE LENGTH
18	6 count Aida / 10 count evenweave	1 7/7" [48 mm]	3/8" [10.0 mm]
20	8 count Aida	1 3/4" [44 mm]	5/16" [9.0 mm]
22	11 count Aida / 22-25-27 count evenweave	1 9/16" [40 mm]	5/16" [8.0 mm]
24	14 count Aida / 28 count evenweave	1 1/2" [36 mm]	9/32" [7.5 mm]
26	16 count Aida / 32 count evenweave	1 5/16" [33 mm]	1/4" [6.5 mm]
28	18 count Aida / 36-55 count evenweave	1 1/16" 28 mm	7/32" [5.5 mm]

EQUIPMENT

Cross stitch uses relatively little equipment, leaving you free to build a collection of the beautiful threads available (see rear cover photograph).

A Needles

B Fabric

C Thread (including tacking thread)

D Dressmaking shears

E Embroidery scissors

F Thimble

G Laying tool: a small pointed stick of metal or wood for smoothing and straightening threads as you stitch (a large blunt-tipped needle will do)

H Masking and double-sided tape

I Embroidery marker pencil

J Embroidery chalk pencil

K Carbon paper for tracing designs

L Graph paper for charting

M Lamp with daylight bulb

N Magnifying glass

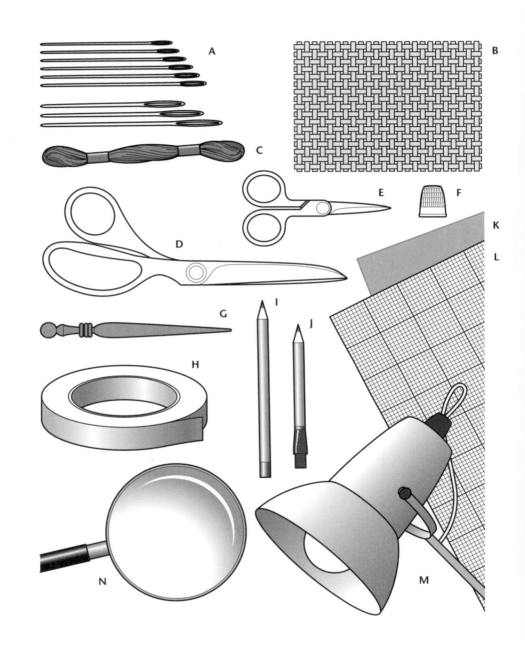

WORKING WITH HOOPS AND FRAMES

Hoops and frames are not essential equipment but they do keep the fabric taut and smooth and make it easier to see how your work is progressing.

Embroidery hoops consist of an inner and an outer ring made of wood or plastic. The fabric is first placed over the inner ring and the outer one is fastened around both by tightening a metal screw.

A hoop or frame can also be mounted on a stand, which then leaves both hands free for stitching. Many people find that stabbing the needle up and down through the fabric, with one hand above and one below, is more comfortable than hand-holding their embroidery, and it helps reduce any pain or cramp in the wrists and fingers.

On the whole, unless your project is quite small-scale, it is better to use a frame than an embroidery hoop. Instead of having to reposition the hoop as you go, the entire work is stretched between two bars.

Hoop marks left on a finished project can be avoided by first wrapping both inner and outer rings with bias binding or by placing tissue paper between the outer ring and the embroidery (tear the tissue away from the stitching area). Remove the hoop when you are not working.

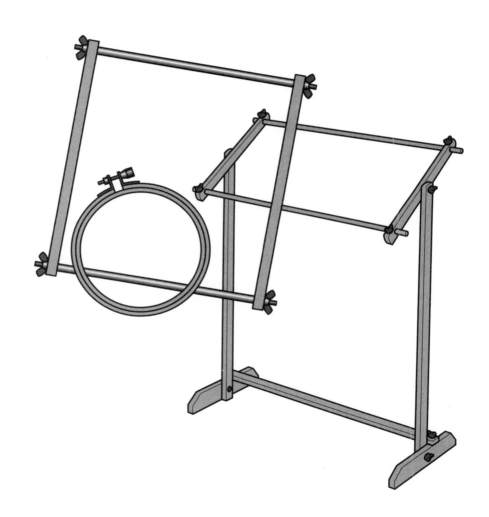

NEEDLES

Cross stitch is worked with blunt-tipped tapestry needles designed to glide through the holes in the fabric weave without splitting the threads. They have long oval eyes (see chart p. 5) that will take multiple strands of embroidery floss as well as craft threads like pearl cotton and tapestry wool. Here are other useful additions to your needle case:

Blunt-tipped

Pointed

Sharps Medium-length pointed needles with a round eye, for general sewing with ordinary cotton or polyester thread.

Embroidery or crewel Pointed like sharps but with long oval eyes like tapestry needles.

Chenille Sharp points and long oval eyes but larger than a crewel, for use on heavy fabrics.

Milliner's needles (also called straws) With round eyes, even shaft and sharp point.

Bodkins Large blunt-tipped needles, sometimes flat, with an eye big enough to take cord, elastic or ribbon through loops and casings.

Eyes are either round or oval; round ones are the smallest and long oval the largest. Although a small needle helps with fine work, if the eye is too tight around the thread or yarn, it will be difficult to pull through the fabric and could fray the thread in the process.

Most needles are nickel plated; however, the quality varies. They sometimes become discolored and may make marks on your work if left stuck in the fabric, so put them away when you have finished. Gold and platinum plated needles will not discolor or rust but they are more expensive.

Some people keep a tiny emery pin cushion packed firmly with sand, which acts as an abrasive to clean the needles when stuck into the cushion.

THREADS

Most embroidery threads can be used in cross stitch. They are available in many forms, in balls, on spools, or in skeins and hanks.

Stranded floss Often called silk and the most commonly used thread. It consists of six divisible strands in a small skein.

Pearl cotton Shiny 2-ply twisted thread. Unlike stranded floss, it cannot be separated into strands. However, it is available in various thicknesses.

Flower thread Thick unmercerized cotton twist and non-divisible like pearl. Its matt finish and soft colors suit antique-style projects like samplers.

Stranded rayon Hi-gloss six-stranded floss.

Z-twist rayon Glossy 4-ply twist, spun clockwise.

Metallic threads A wide range to choose from. Slightly abrasive, tending to fray at the ends, these call for a large-eyed needle to make a bigger hole in the cloth and reduce the drag on both thread and fabric. For this reason it is best to work with short lengths.

Space-dyed (or variegated) threads Factory-dyed in multiple colors, or in shades of a single color, at regular intervals along the thread.

Hand-dyed threads Dyed by hand using one or more colors, possibly neither light- nor color-fast.

Choose threads in natural light because artificial lighting intensifies certain colors and dulls others. The fibers that you choose are equally important for the texture or finish of your embroidery and you should always bear in mind the end use of whatever you make.

You can buy shade cards, including actual thread samples, from major manufacturers. They are also obtainable from online needlecraft suppliers.

When using a twist thread, always thread your needle directly from the ball before cutting off the length required. This ensures that the twist of the thread goes in the same direction every time, giving an even appearance to your stitches.

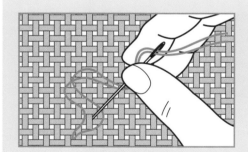

Railroading is the technique of separating and smoothing strands of thread as you stitch. As you push your needle into the fabric to make a stitch, pass it between two strands.

FABRICS AND THREAD COUNTS

The background texture and color provided by your fabric is important. The most widely used fabrics for cross stitch are evenweave and Aida, and both come in ranges of neutral tones and colors.

Aida

This block weave fabric is favored by beginners because of its regular construction and visible stitch holes. It also has a stiffer finish for hand-held work. It is worth noting that unworked areas have a distinct texture compared with evenweave.

If the pattern contains fractional stitches (p. 22), you will have to make an additional hole between the existing ones by stitching into the solid section of the block weave.

5-, 6- or 8-count A low-count Aida for use by children, sometimes called Binca canvas.

11-count Many find that they can work on this when the more usual 14-count becomes too hard on the eyes. Good beginner fabric.

14-count Easy to work and used in more commercial designs than any other fabric. Beginner fabric.

16-count Gives scope for greater detail than 14-count. Intermediate fabric.

18-count An Aida for detailed work. Stitch a small sample before launching upon a large project as you may find this count too demanding for comfort. Intermediate fabric.

22 -count Another Aida for really fine work. Traditionally used for Hardanger and also ideal for small projects such as pot lids, paperweights and coasters. Advanced fabric.

Canvas

You can cross stitch with tapestry wool or stranded floss on a cotton or linen canvas. There are four mesh sizes, 10-, 12-, 14- and 18-count, which are compatible with any stitch chart (count the holes in canvas work, not the threads). With a starched finish that gives a firm base to work on, canvas comes as both single thread mesh (mono) and double (duo).

The latter is also called Penelope canvas, which can be used to double your count and—like evenweave—simplifies fractional stitches. Ease the double threads apart first with a thick tapestry needle, then treat each as a single.

Plastic canvas

Plastic mesh is available in circles as well as straight-sided sheets. It is usually stitched with 4-ply or worsted wool over counts of 5, 7, 10 or 14 holes to the inch (2.5 cm). Being rigid, it can be pre-cut for making into items such as boxes, place mats, Christmas decorations, photo frames and key holders.

Evenweave

An evenweave is any natural or man-made fabric having the same number of threads per inch (2.5 cm) counted vertically and horizontally; this keeps the cross stitches square and even. It is frequently made either of linen, such as Belfast (32-count) and Cashel (28-count) or—less expensively—of cotton, such as Linda (27-count) and Hardanger (22-count).

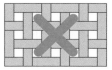

Evenweave threads are usually of uniform thickness, though the pure linens are more random. Cross stitch is worked over two threads, so you will be stitching into alternate holes.

The *greater the thread count* per inch, sometimes given as HPI (holes per inch), the *finer the cloth* and the *smaller your stitches* will be. A 22-count evenweave will yield 11 cross stitches per inch and a 32-count produces 16.

Evenweave and Aida are interchangeable with the aid of a little arithmetic. So if a pattern calls for 28-count evenweave stitched over 2 threads of the fabric, use a 14-count Aida and stitch into every hole instead. In the same way, you would replace 32-count evenweave with 16-count Aida, and 22-count with 11-count.

Both fabrics are woven in a variety of widths and also in narrow bands with pre-stitched edges, suitable for bookmarks, cakebands, tie-backs and so on. The bands are 1¾–3 in [3–8 cm] in width.

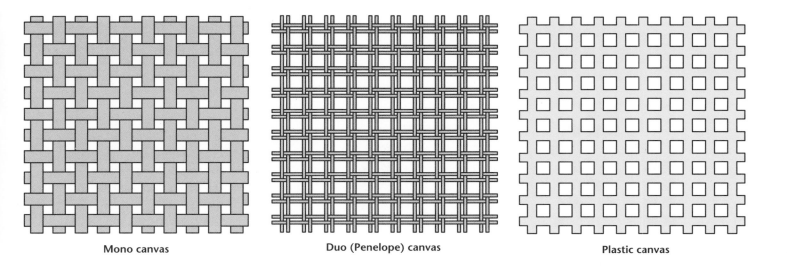

Mono canvas   Duo (Penelope) canvas   Plastic canvas

CALCULATING QUANTITIES

When calculating the amount of fabric you need for a project, add a clear margin of 4–5 in [10–12 cm] around the outer edges of the design. Allow proportionally less if the design itself is no bigger than a 4–5 in [10–12 cm] square.

A skein of embroidery floss is approximately 25 feet [7.5 m] long. On average, people work with an 18 in [45 cm] length of floss at a time. You will get roughly 16 working lengths of 6 strands' thickness from one skein and twice as many with it split into 3 strands. It is wise to discount one of those lengths for starting and finishing and general wastage.

CROSS STITCH CHARTS AND HOW TO READ THEM

Pattern books became very popular in Europe and America during the seventeenth century. In the early days, cross stitch patterns had only plain black squares or dots, with no color guide. Now there is a variety of squared charts, from those that use only symbols for colors to those printed in full color.

Here is a very simple heart-shaped motif. Each square on the chart represents two threads of evenweave fabric or one block of Aida, and each stitch occupies one square.

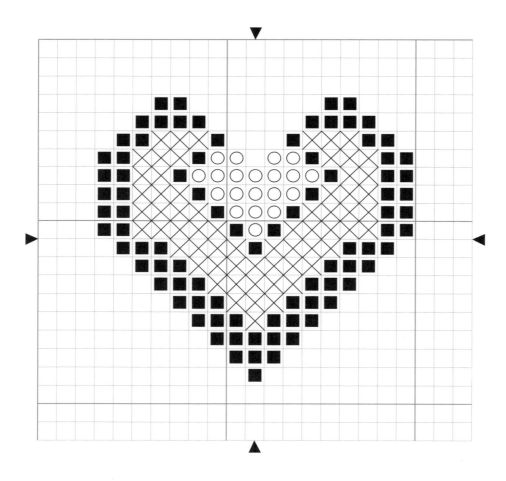

Design size 17w x 16h

Stitching level Beginner

Always mark the center of each edge of the chart with a small arrowhead. Even so, it can be difficult to keep your place on a large chart. Try dividing it into a grid of manageable sections, marked with a colored pen (see also p. 19).

Small symbols in one corner of a square stand for either a quarter-stitch or three-quarter stitch (see p. 22) and these two can also be combined within the same square. In that case, the chart will show a square divided by a diagonal. The half-stitch is generally used for shading or to lighten a color.

■ red   ✕ blue   ○ yellow

CHARTING YOUR OWN DESIGN

Being able to chart your own design broadens your cross-stitching horizons considerably. The choice of subjects is limitless and with practice you will develop the knack of visualizing a finished item. Graph paper is essential. If you haven't any, you can scan or photocopy basic grids like those provided overleaf, or download graph paper in various count sizes from online needlecraft sites.

It is the number of stitches from top to bottom and side to side that fix the design size; do not forget to include any stitched background area in your calculations. Start by outlining the required number of squares on your chart. For a 12 in (30 cm) design, you will work to 168 (12x14) stitches on 14-count Aida. There will be fewer stitches on 11-count: 132 (12x11) and many more stitches on 18-count: 216 (12x18).

Remember that *evenweave is worked over two threads so divide the evenweave thread count by two* before you begin to calculate the number of stitches required.

You can either color in your chart or, if you are charting in black and white, decide on a system of symbols as a key to the colors.

Cross-stitched initials vary a lot in width or depth according to the letters of the alphabet. Capitals G, M, Q, R and W are the ones to watch out for, particularly if you are working to tight margins such as a key holder or bookmark.

Digital chartmaking

If you want to create a chart via your computer and you have the necessary software, the graphics program Adobe Photoshop can be used to convert a photograph to a counted cross-stitch pattern. There are also online charts of leading thread manufacturers' colors for you to choose from.

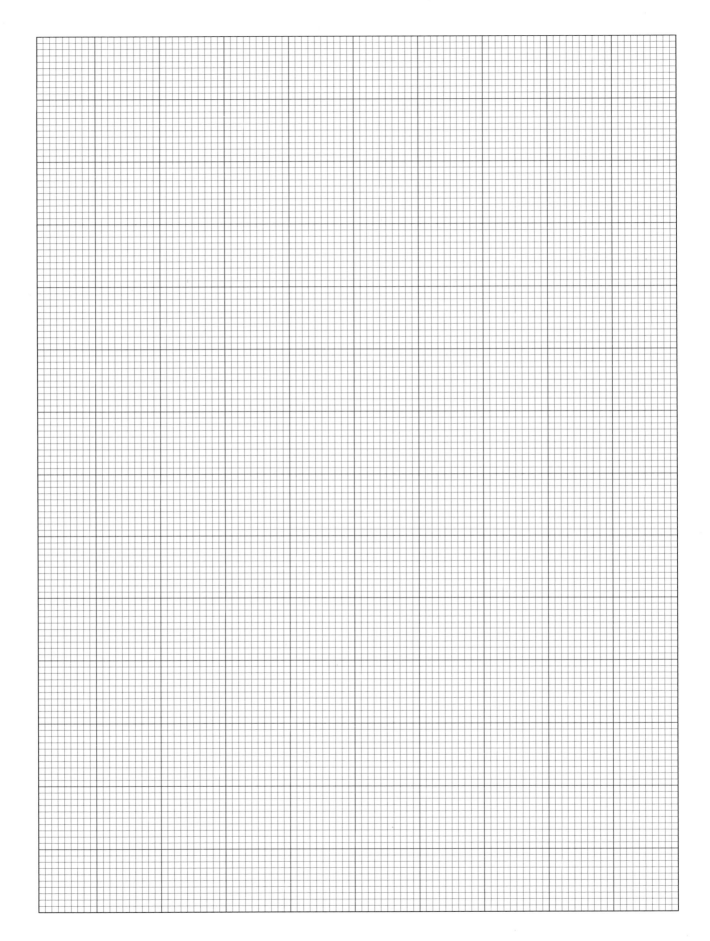

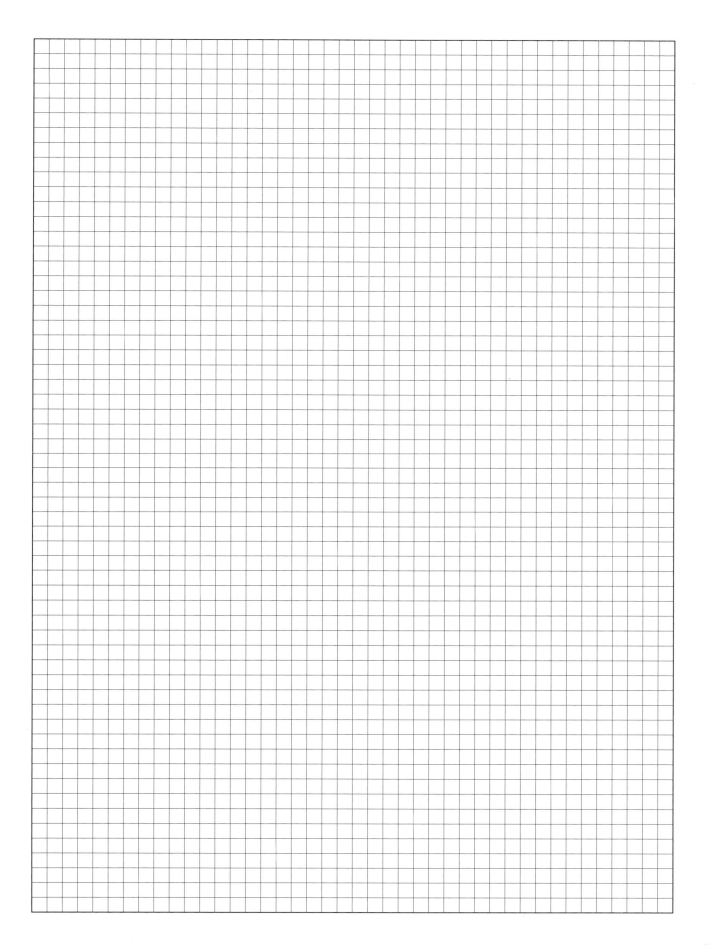

READYMADES

There are many manufactured items that you can buy from needlecraft suppliers to decorate with cross stitch, including plastic canvas for you to cut and construct to your own designs (and ideas for box shapes as below, see p. 38).

Small objects like key holders, pot lids and tasselled scissor keepers are a very encouraging way of starting—and finishing—a project (see p. 39). As gift items they can be given the personal touch of initials or a favorite motto, or stitched to match a particular color scheme. Kits are also available for brooches, wallets, coasters, fridge magnets, handbag mirrors, paperweights, pendants and pin cushions.

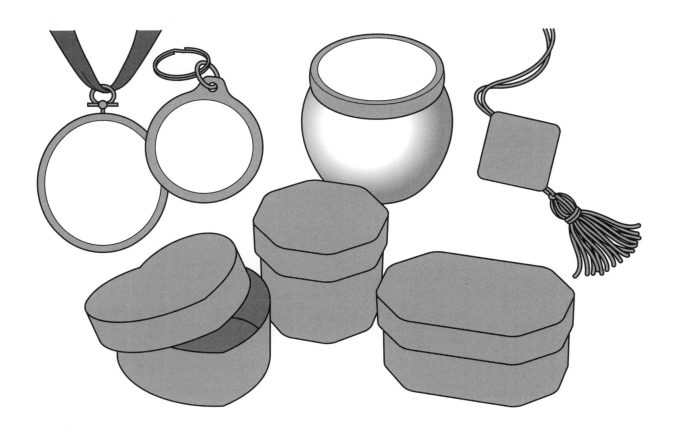

PART TWO:
CROSS STITCH METHODS AND TECHNIQUES

THREAD ORGANIZER

At the start of a project, punch a line of holes in a piece of card and loop a 3 in [7 cm] strand from each skein through a separate hole. Write the name of the project in the center of the card and then label each hole with the appropriate manufacturer's name, shade number and chart symbol. This provides you with a quick reference while you work and a handy record once you have finished.

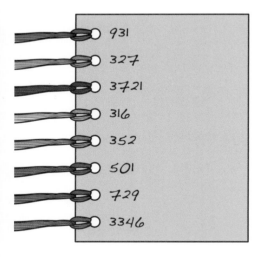

PREPARING FABRIC

Keep fabrics in a sealed bag or box and wash your hands before handling. When you have cut a new piece—removing any selvages in the process—check it carefully for faults in the weave and then iron it smooth under a clean, dry cloth (an old sheet will do). Stubborn creases may require steaming.

Prepare the raw edges

Linen frays very easily, so does evenweave, Aida less so. But whatever fabric you use, you should prepare the raw edges in order to keep them neat and prevent your threads getting caught while you embroider. Here are some options:

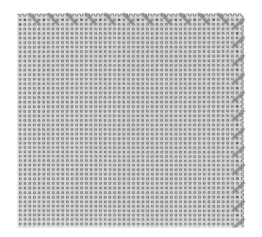

1 Overstitch around the edges by hand with sewing cotton, even roll a small hem if you wish.

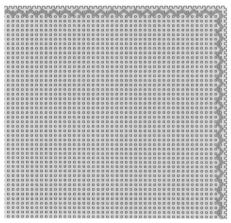

2 Zigzag stitch round the edges with a sewing machine.

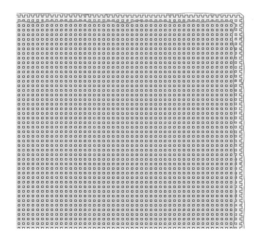

3 Apply an anti-fray fluid sparingly and allow to dry before working.

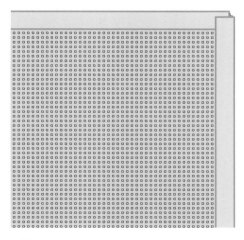

4 Frame with masking tape.

With 3 and 4, be aware that you will have to cut away ½ in [1 cm] all round afterwards. Chemicals and adhesives will damage the fabric in the long run.

Basting guidelines

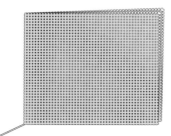

1 Fold the fabric in half twice to find the center point, crease gently with your fingers and mark with a pin.

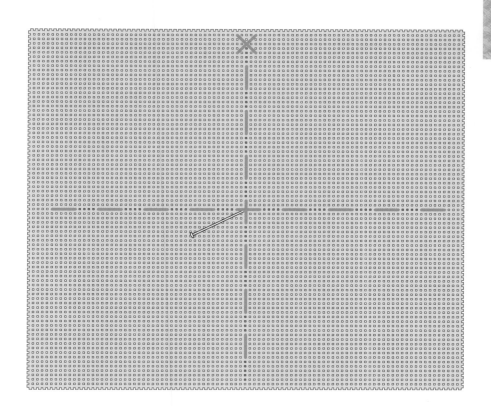

2 Open out and baste along the folds in a contrasting thread; this stitching corresponds to the colored guidelines on your chart (p. 12). Use soft cotton basting thread if possible because it is easier to remove.

Choose a place outside your stitching area and sew a large X to indicate the right side of the work and mark the top.

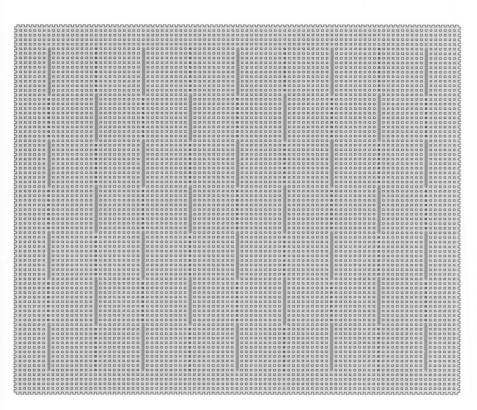

Grid making

In addition to marking the two central lines with basting thread, you could go further and baste an entire grid based on squares of 10x10. This is worth considering if you are starting a large project since you will save time and be able to orientate yourself more easily, even working one color at a time right through the design. The chances of counting errors are reduced because you never have to count more than ten up, down or across.

You will already have the 10x10 grid marked on your chart for cross reference (p. 12).

PREPARING THREADS

How many strands to use

As a rule, the number of strands of floss that you sew with should match the thickness of one thread pulled out from the edge of the fabric. People generally use three or four strands on an 11-count fabric, two or three for a 14-count, and two for an 18-count.

Single strand outline

Many pictorial cross stitch designs are outlined in backstitch. This is often sewn in black (not to be confused with blackwork, p. 23) with just one or two strands of floss.

Separating and recombining stranded floss

Multiple strands of floss used straight from the skein can produce bumpy stitches so it is worth taking the trouble to separate the strands, smooth them straight and put them together again *in the same direction*. This will reduce twisting and tangling, and the stitches will lie better.

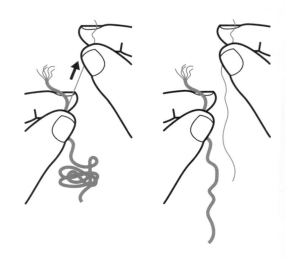

Grip one strand firmly at the top and draw your other hand down, taking the remaining threads with you until the single strand is free. The others will bunch up but won't become knotted. Finally, lay all the strands out straight and reassemble them as you wish.

Tweeding

Different colored strands threaded into the same needle is known as tweeding. Achieved by separating strands (see above), it is a good way of introducing textural effects and also of creating extra colors without buying more; for instance, blue and pink strands will produce mauve. There is also a very fine metallic thread, known as a blending filament designed for combination with ordinary stranded floss.

The blending filament and stranded floss will not slip when the filament is threaded up as shown. The floss is threaded up afterwards in the usual way.

Thread organizer

As well as creating a record card (p. 17), well-organized stitchers might like to make a similar one for use throughout the project. Cut a thread of each color to a working length (about 18 in [45 cm]) and loop it through the punched card, where it remains ready for the needle.

Metallic threads tend to twist or break more easily, so it is advisable to cut those into shorter lengths (about 12 in [30 cm]). They also tend to unravel at the ends, which can be stopped with anti-fray fluid. Ends can be prepared in advance on the thread organizer and eventually trimmed off.

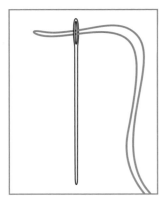

1 Loop the filament and thread it into the needle.

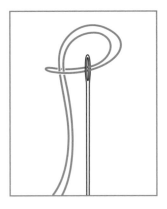

2 Thread the free ends through the loop.

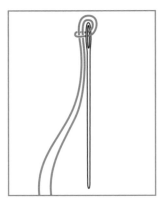

3 Pull the ends of the filament very gently to secure it in the eye of the needle.

STARTING AND FASTENING OFF

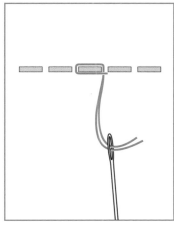

Unless the design demands otherwise, stitch from the center and work outward, counting the squares as you go. Unless you have basted a grid (p. 19), plan your progress to avoid long empty stretches because that's where you run the risk of miscounting. Also, carrying threads very far across the back tends to show through.

No knots

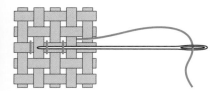

Knots at the back will appear as unsightly bumps on the front of your work when it is finally pressed and mounted. They will even pop right through the weave if it is loose enough. So, when starting out, push your needle through from the wrong side leaving a 1.5 in [3 cm] tail of thread at the back. Hold the tail against the fabric as you go and it will soon be caught down by the new stitches.

The correct way to fasten off is to run the thread under three or four wrong-side stitches, either horizontally or vertically. Whipping the end around one of those stitches helps to secure it.

Waste knots

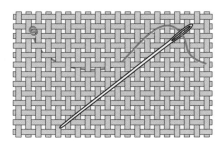

First knot the end of the thread and from the *right side* push your needle through to the back, leaving the knot on the surface of the fabric. Next, bring your needle through again about 1 in [2.5 cm] from the knot and start stitching toward it. Stab stitch steadily and be sure to completely cover the thread at the back. When that is done, trim the knot from the front.

An "Away Waste Knot" is placed well away from the stitching and is not covered by it. When cut off, it leaves a longer tail at the back, which is threaded into a needle and woven in.

The loop start or lark's head knot

Two conditions hold for this method: first, working with an even number of strands of floss; and second, the working length of thread should be doubled to 36 in (90 cm).

Separate one strand of floss if you are stitching with two strands (two for four, and three for six). Fold the strand(s) double and thread the loose ends into your needle.

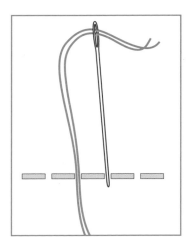

1 Stab the needle up through the fabric from the wrong to the right side and pull enough thread with it to leave a small loop at the back.

2 Make your first half cross stitch and, with the needle back on the wrong side, pass it through the waiting loop.

3 As you pull the thread it will draw the loop neatly against the fabric.

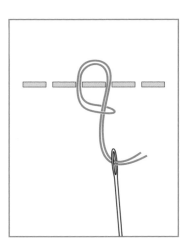

BASIC STITCHES

Cross stitch

The most important rule about cross stitch is that all the top stitches go in one direction. It doesn't matter which way as long as they are uniform. Working with separated and recombined strands (p. 20), railroading (p. 9) and smoothing your stitches with a laying tool will help.

There are two cross-stitching methods.

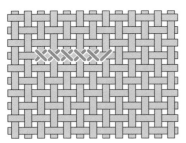

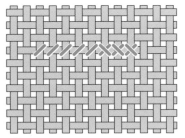

1 The traditional English method completes each X before moving on to the next.

2 The Danish method does the first legs of the Xs first, and completes them as they return along the row.

To end with all the threads in neat vertical lines on the back, stitch horizontal rows with the Danish method and vertical columns with the English.

There are also two styles of stitching. One is the stabbing or push and pull method. There is no alternative when working with a hoop or frame because the fabric is too taut. But if hand-holding, you can manipulate the fabric to use the sewing method below.

Fractional stitches

These are quarter, half and three-quarter cross stitches, mainly used to smooth outlines and round corners. However, they can give a lighter look to an otherwise solid area, or share a square with another color, in a variation on tweeding.

The half-stitch is the same as the first leg of the Danish method shown left.

The quarter-stitch is done across one thread only if you are working on evenweave fabric; on Aida it must be done as shown right.

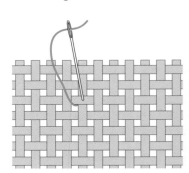

Coming up from the lower left corner, cross diagonally and insert the needle into the solid center of the Aida square. Pull the thread right through to the back.

The three-quarter-stitch on Aida fabric takes the first step as for the quarter-stitch above and finishes as shown right.

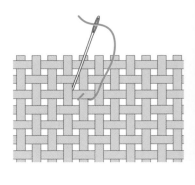

Coming up from the lower right corner, cross diagonally and insert the needle into the hole top left. Pull the thread right through to the back.

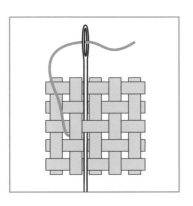

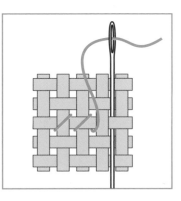

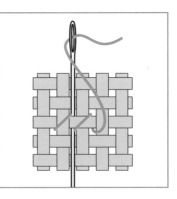

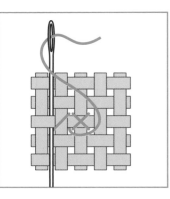

1 On the first leg, in one action, push the needle into the fabric at the top and out of the hole below.

2 Repeat for the remainder of the row.

3 Cross the last stitch diagonally, pushing the needle in at the top and out of the hole directly below.

4 Repeat to the other end of the row where all the crosses will be complete.

Backstitch

The backstitch has close links with cross stitch. It is used to define cross-stitched areas and should be done last in order to maintain an unbroken line. Some stitchers prefer to use a finer needle at this stage—it is a thin line and the number of strands is seldom more than one or two. Most often a single strand is used but it does not always have to be black; in fact, you may achieve a far more subtle and pleasing effect with a darker shade of the cross stitch filler. Start and finish by running the thread under a few cross stitches at the back of your project.

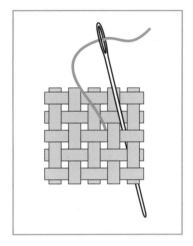 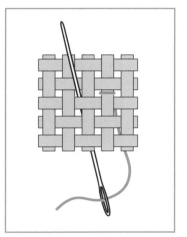 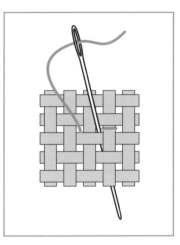 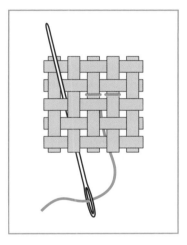

1 Push the needle in one stitch space *behind* the point where it previously came out.

2 Bring the needle back out one stitch space *in front* of the previous stitch.

3 Push it in again at the point where the previous stitch ended.

4 And bring it out one stitch space ahead of the latest stitch.

Holbein or Double Running Stitch

This is a staple stitch of blackwork. It looks like backstitch but is actually constructed from two passes of running stitch, where the second pass returns and precisely fills the gaps left by the first. This makes the back far neater than that of backstitch and ideal on its own for double-sided items such as bookmarks and Christmas tree decorations.

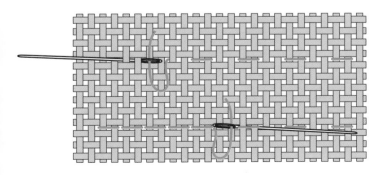

Blackwork

A type of decorative stitching believed to have been brought to England from Spain by Henry VIII's first wife, Catherine of Aragon. It eventually developed into the English style of sections outlined in double running stitch and filled with extremely complex geometric patterns. The original thread was waxed black silk and although other colors were sometimes used—occasionally red or gold-wrapped—they were seldom used together. Blackwork fell out of fashion for clothing but persisted on samplers. Today, blackwork often incorporates one or two secondary colors.

THE HISTORY OF SAMPLERS

The word "sampler" is derived from the French "examplaire" meaning a model to be copied. Samplers were the forerunners of printed patterns, collections of stitches and motifs for sewing on to household linens and clothes. The earliest reference is recorded in 1502 on a bill of accounts for Elizabeth of York, wife of the English king Henry VII: "for an elne (*sic*) of lynnyn cloth for a sampler for the Quene." An ell measured 45 in or 115 cm.

Early English samplers were sewn on narrow linen strips, about 6–9 in [15– 23 cm] wide cut across the width of the loom on which they were woven. Cloth was very expensive and designs were worked into every spare fiber. They displayed a huge variety of stitches in as many as twenty different colors of silk and metal threads.

Germany produced the first printed pattern book in 1523 and by the end of the century every other European country had followed suit. The oldest surviving sampler was signed and dated by Jane Bostocke of England in 1598 and certainly shows the influence of such patterns.

During the next century it became fashionable to add a border of geometric or floral design and from about 1650 moral inscriptions

were included. The idea of the sampler as an educational tool had arrived and it then became a record of virtue and achievement.

Throughout the 1700s, samplers changed to a square format and into highly ornamental pictures, maps, and even mathematical tables, all of which were intended to show off the needleworker's skill in the craft.

By the end of the nineteenth century and the close of the Victorian era, the craze for the needlework motto had taken over. Pre-printed on perforated paper and sold for pennies, it usually featured a domestic or rural scene and a proverb or quotation from the Bible. Cross stitch was the dominant stitch and schoolchildren and hobbyists everywhere could produce very satisfying results.

Four traditional sampler motifs: a tree, a dog, a man and a house.

BACKSTITCH ALPHABET

A sampler-style alphabet with matching numerals, designed to be executed in backstitch using just two strands of embroidery floss. This alphabet is also suitable for lettering tiny keepsake items or for signing and dating your own work.

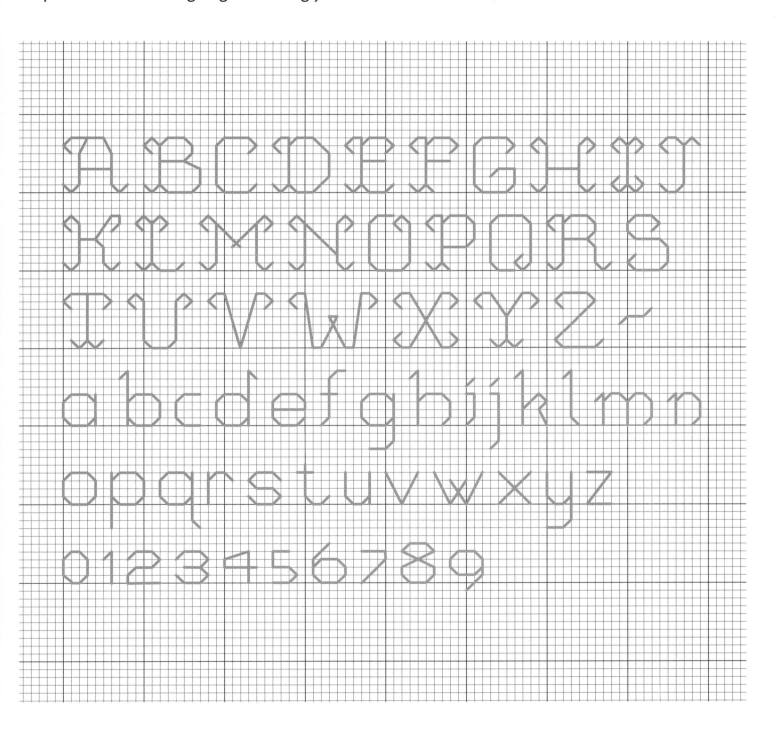

POPULAR SAMPLER MOTIFS

This page contains 15 popular motifs on a standard 10x10 grid for easy counting. Those with a backstitch outline can be worked without one, if you wish. Stitch them in one single color or many, the choice is yours. And you can make them singly or combine them into pictures.

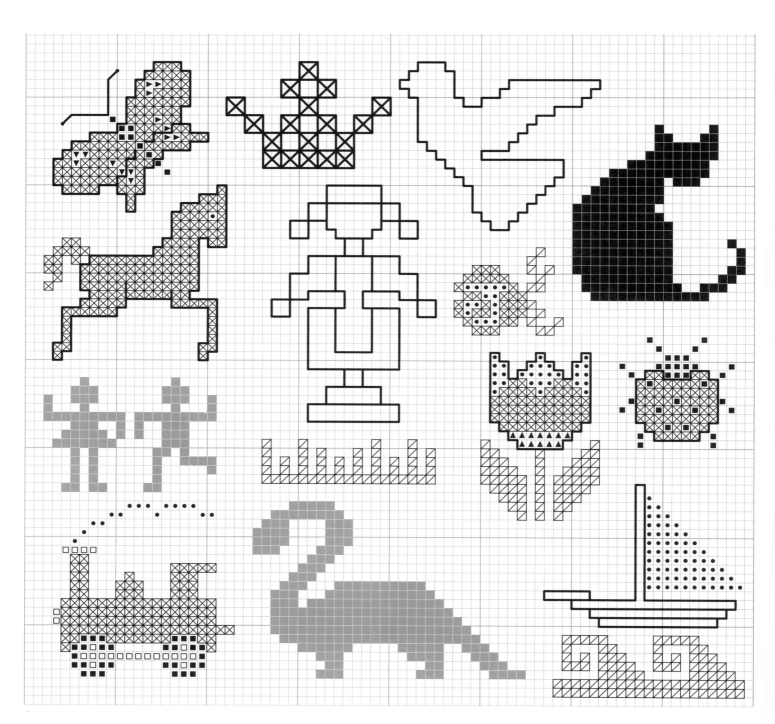

ASSISI WORK

Assisi work is a thirteenth-century embroidery technique from the Italian town of the same name. It consists of a voided (i.e. blank) motif, outlined in backstitch or Holbein stitch, and surrounded by a background of solid cross stitch (for a range of cross stitch variations, see pp. 30–31).

Originally, nuns embroidered these designs on church altar cloths, working on plain linen in two colors of silk thread. The outline was usually stitched in black, with red or blue for the background filling; later, brown, green and gold were introduced.

Formal subjects suit Assisi work best, like heraldic beasts and mythical creatures. Traditionally, the creatures were arranged in symmetrical pairs between intricate borders worked in the same color as the background.

To embroider a reproduction version, you will need a high-count cream linen evenweave (28-count or higher). You could dip it briefly in weak black tea to give it an antique look. Do not wring it; let it drip dry naturally and press before use. Experiment with the number of strands of thread to produce the effect you want but keep to the traditional colors. If you are using an antiqued fabric, you will probably find softer shades look more authentic.

Of course, you can take the Assisi style and give it a more contemporary treatment with variegated threads or colored evenweave fabric, and the motifs don't have to be traditional either.

HERALDIC BEASTS AND MYTHICAL CREATURES

A page of fantastic creatures set on a standard 10x10 grid. These are easily adapted for Assisi-style projects by voiding the patterned squares, outlining them in Holbein stitch, and cross stitching the background instead. For the characteristic filigree borders found on Assisi work, see the example on the previous page or turn to p. 40.

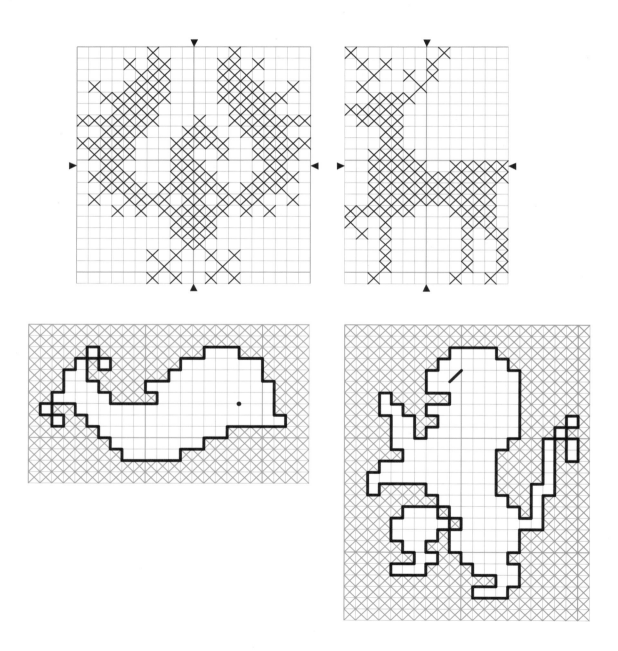

ASSISI-STYLE ALPHABET

These decorative initials are in marked contrast to the backstitch alphabet on p. 25.
The letters may be voided from the background, like Assisi work.

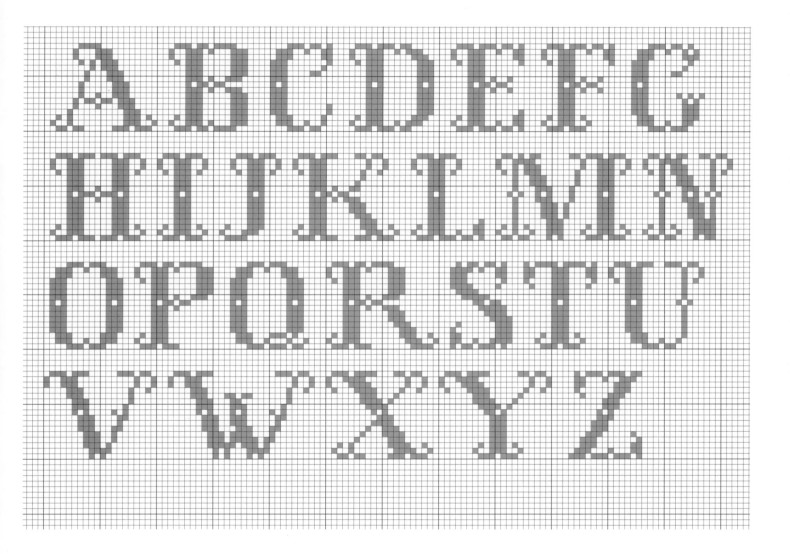

CROSS STITCH VARIATIONS

These diagrams show examples worked on evenweave fabric. For Aida, halve the number of threads in the instructions and substitute squares. All of these stitches can be worked larger or smaller by increasing or decreasing the number of threads or squares that you work over.

Herringbone stitch

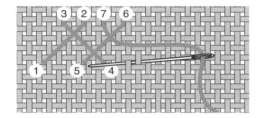

Stitch a diagonal 4 threads right and 4 threads up. Needle in at top and out 2 threads left. Stitch diagonal 4 threads right and 4 threads down. Needle in at base and out 2 threads left. Repeat to form a row, following the numbered points.

Threaded herringbone stitch

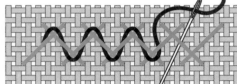

Work a row of herringbone stitch. Secure second color thread on wrong side by whipping round existing stitches. Bring needle through and weave in and out of herringbone without stitching into fabric. Needle in and fasten off on wrong side.

Long-armed cross stitch

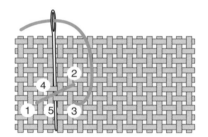

1 Following the numbers, stitch a long diagonal right. Needle in at top and out again below. Cross over previous stitch. Once again, needle in at top and out below.

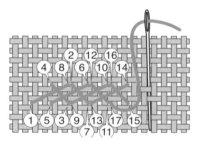

2 Repeat to form a row, following the numbered points. Repeated rows make a bold background filling, especially for Assisi work.

Tied cross stitch

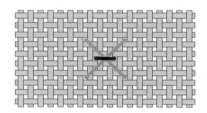

Work a cross stitch over 4 threads. Bring needle through, level with center. Stitch across over 2 threads. Work a foundation row of cross stitch, then stitch central ties with a row of running stitch in a second color.

Algerian eye stitch

1 Bring needle through at left base and work 8 straight stitches clockwise into the same central hole, following the numbered points.

2 Pull stitches firmly to create the central hole. Do not allow threads on wrong side to cover it.

Smyrna (double cross) stitch

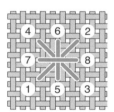

Bring needle through at left base. Stitch a diagonal 4 threads right and 4 threads up. Needle in at top and out 4 threads directly below. Work 3 more straight stitches, each over 4 threads, as numbered.

Boxed cross stitch

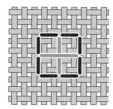

Work a vertical cross stitch over 4 threads. Box in with a square formation of 8 backstitch or Holbein stitches over 2 threads each.

Open filling stitch

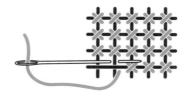

Work a grid of long, evenly spaced straight stitches. Bring needle through at each intersection and work a cross stitch over 2 or 3 threads. The cross ties can be a second color. This is a good filler for blackwork.

Woven (braided) cross

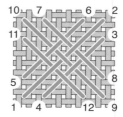

Bring needle through at left base. Stitch a diagonal 8 threads right and 8 threads up. Needle in at top and out 2 threads directly below. Work 3 more straight stitches, as numbered, before weaving the final 3 stitches in and out of the first set.

Tied half Rhodes stitch

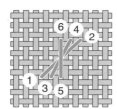

1 Bring needle through at left base. Stitch a diagonal 4 threads right and 4 threads up. Needle in at top and out 1 thread further right along base. Work 2 more straight stitches, following the numbered points, ending with a vertical.

2 Stitch 2 more diagonals across the vertical, following the numbered points.

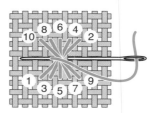

3 Bring needle through, level with center point. Stitch across over 2 threads.

Rice stitch

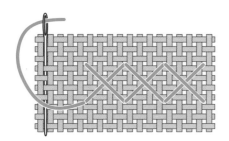

1 Bring needle through at base. Stitch a diagonal 4 threads right and 4 threads up. Needle in at top and out 4 threads directly below. Repeat to form a row, then return, completing the crosses.

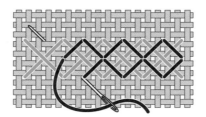

2 In a second color, backstitch over each half leg of each cross stitch. The backstitches are worked over 2 threads.

3 Rice stitch forms an effective background for contemporary Assisi work.

"Sans" is French for "without," and letters without serifs do not have the little bracket-like features found at the ends of vertical and horizontal strokes in a serif alphabet (see opposite).

SERIF ALPHABET PLUS NUMERALS

KNOT STITCHES

Knots are indicated on charts by filled-in dots. The knot family plays a significant part in counted cross stitch, being ideal for tiny details on flowers and faces. However, people often have more trouble with these small stitches than any others. They need practice, no doubt, but it is also vital to use the correct needle. Tapestry needles have fat eyes that do not make good coils; a fine, smooth, sharp embroidery needle is best.

French knot

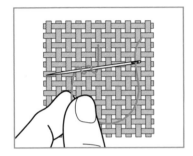 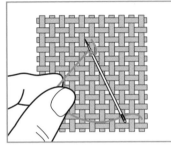 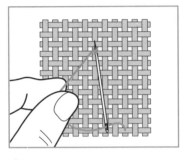 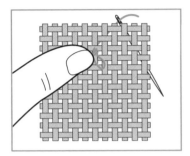

1 Wrap the thread around the needle as many times as the pattern requires.

2 Holding the needle in one hand, pull the thread gently until the coils tighten and start sliding down toward the tip.

3 Insert the needle close to where the thread originally came out. On evenweave, the distance is one thread; on Aida, the next square. Avoid using the same hole or the knot will disappear to the wrong side.

4 With a firm grasp on the fabric, press down with your thumb to hold the coils in place and pull the needle and thread gently but firmly through to the other side, leaving a perfect knot on the surface.

Four-legged knot

This knot can be used singly or as a filling stitch. It looks good either upright or on the diagonal.

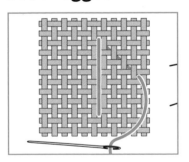 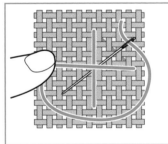 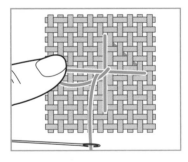 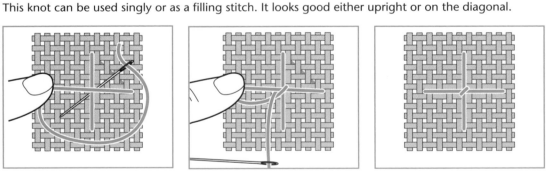

1 Make a vertical stitch over 8 threads. Needle in at top and out 4 threads below and 4 threads right, ready for the arms of the cross.

2 Hold thread across the mid-vertical with your thumb while sliding the needle diagonally from top right to base left. The looped thread hangs below the vertical stitch.

3 Pull needle and thread down carefully through the loop to form a knot and tighten it around the center of the vertical.

4 Needle in 4 threads left, level with knot, to complete the cross.

PART THREE:

STITCHABLES

TEMPLATES

Stitchables include readymades (see p.16) and any items that you may have made yourself— like an apron, bag or cushion— or bought specially to embroider, such as a baby's bib, table runner or pillow cases.

Trace, copy or scan these templates for use as stitched borders, picture mounts or framed greetings cards. Cut them out carefully from paper or thin cardboard with small pointed scissors or a craft knife (always cut away from your other hand, never toward it).

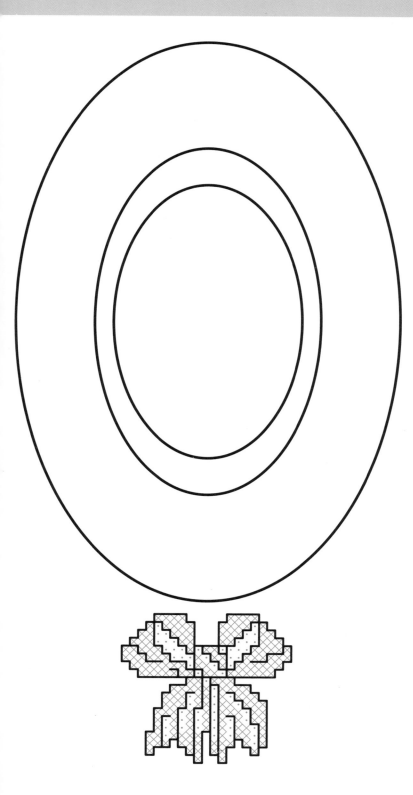

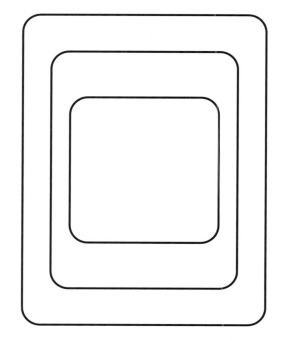

GREETINGS CARDS

Important occasions deserve to be marked with cards that people will treasure. Even for regular events like birthdays and New Year, hand-embroidered greetings send a special message.

adhesive

centrefold of finished card

opening

fold this section in

Folded card mounts

Open the prepared card and place it face down on a clean sheet of paper. Position your work over the opening, using the basting guidelines (p. 19) to center it. Trim fabric margins to fit inside the card and remove basting. Prepare the adhesive area with double-sided tape or fabric glue. Reposition the embroidery. If required, add tape or glue to the edges of the left-hand section before folding it over to conceal the back of the embroidery. Press down firmly.

A light box is not only handy for tracing designs; use it to position your work quickly and accurately when mounting and framing. No light box? If you have a glass-topped table, simply stand a lamp underneath it and your work surface is transformed.

DECORATIVE BANDS

Both evenweave and Aida are available in narrow bands with pre-stitched edges, and in a growing range of colors (see rear cover photograph).

Measuring 1½–4 ¾ in [3.5–12 cm] wide, these bands can be made into a variety of things, from curtain ties and cake bands to belts and small purses. Turn the raw ends over and line the finished work with broad ribbon, ironed onto the back with fusible web. For a firmer edge, the band and ribbon may be satin-stitched together by hand or machine.

Bookmarks

Create a classic bookmark with decorative initials using the alphabet below or on p. 29. First, baste your guidelines (p. 19), remembering to allow for turnings both ends. For a pointed end, fold the corners up to meet center back in a triangle. Slip stitch together before pressing the lining into place. Finally, sew a tassel (p. 39) to the point.

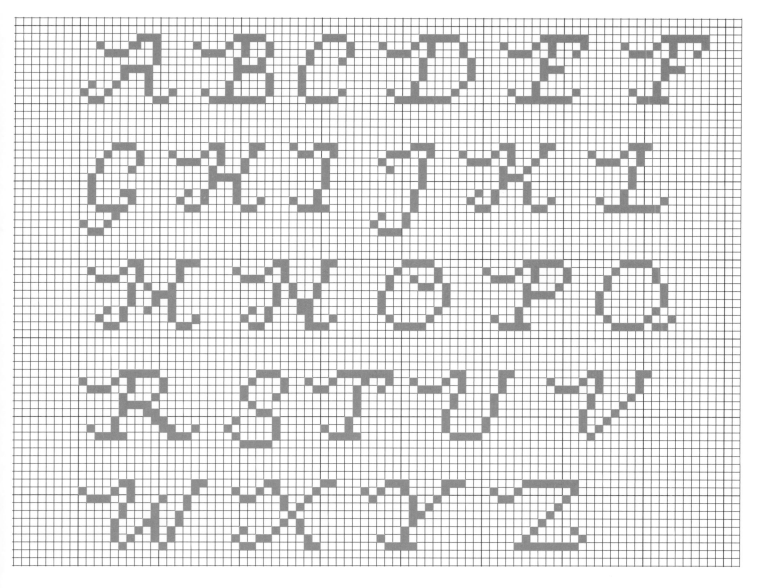

WORKING WITH PLASTIC CANVAS

Plastic canvas is ideal for three-dimensional projects because it is easy to cut to shape, ready to stitch. All you need is a sharp pair of scissors and some bright ideas.

The canvas (p. 11) is produced in various colors and "clear." Unless a background color is part of your design, use the clear plastic. It comes in three forms: standard, rigid and soft. The rigid is good for stand-alone objects like frames and boxes, while the soft makes flexible items such as bangles and bag handles. Of the four mesh sizes, 7-count is the most popular, often worked with worsted wool. Alternatively, use thick pearl cotton or 12 strands of embroidery floss with a 16 or 18 needle.

Festive decorations

Draft the shapes onto standard canvas with a water-soluble marker. Cut the mesh and trim off the nubs; mistakes can be mended with superglue. Wash the shape to remove the ink before stitching. Combine blending filament (see rear cover photograph) with the main thread for a shimmering effect, or use lurex yarn. When you finally blanket-stitch (p. 43) round the edges, add glass beads for extra sparkle.

Make hangers from narrow ribbon or twist your own cord (right). Cut two lengths of rayon or metallic embroidery thread, four times as long as the desired cord. Knot together at both ends and ask someone to hold one end while you slot a pencil through the other. Pull the loop taut between you and start twisting. When you've done enough, the cord will curl up as you relax the tension. Place your finger halfway, release one end and allow it to twist on itself to make the full cord. Smooth out any kinks between thumb and forefinger. Secure with a knot.

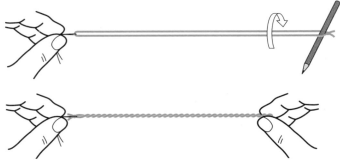

MINIATURE DESIGNS

Small-scale embroidery will fit many of the readymade items available from craft suppliers and is a good way of utilizing scraps of fabric and embroidery threads.

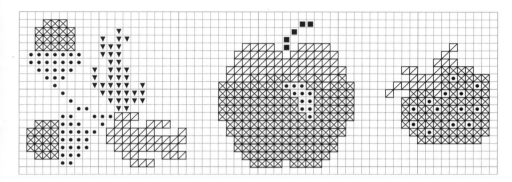

Scissor keeper

Embroider two 2 ½ in [65 mm] squares of Aida and press face down. Put right sides together and backstitch (p. 23) around three sides, with a ¼ in [6 mm] seam allowance. Clip the corners and turn right side out. Stuff the cushion with some wadding and, before closing with blanket stitch (p. 43), insert both ends of a 16 in [40 cm] length of cord at one corner. Blanket stitch (p. 43) around all four sides. Make a tassel (see below) and sew it to the corner diagonally opposite the cord. Finally, loop the cord through one scissor handle.

Trinket pots, pendants and fobs

Stitch your miniatures on 16- to 22-count Aida, with two strands in a 26 or 28 needle. Readymades usually carry a cardboard insert; draw crosslines on it like the guidelines on your work (p. 19). Align centers by sticking a pin through both, then draw lightly around the cardboard. Cut the fabric out along the line and remove the basting. Iron the embroidery face down, place inside the item, and seal.

Tassels

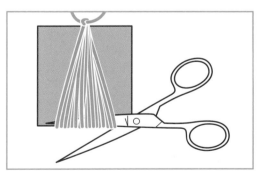

1 Wrap the thread around the cardboard. Thread one strand, 12 in [30 cm] long, under the top loops.

2 Tie this strand tightly at the top; the ends can be knotted or twisted later, or threaded up for sewing. Cut all the tassel loops free at the lower edge.

3 Take another length of thread and wind firmly round the loose strands to form the tassel head. Finish with a secure knot. Thread the ends into a needle and work neatly into the center of the tassel before trimming level.

BORDERS AND CORNERS

An essential feature of samplers and Assisi work, borders are worked once the main design is complete. Clever use of color can create a three-dimensional effect. Only one or two strands of thread are required for a fine-line backstitch border.

PART FOUR:
BASIC EMBROIDERY STITCHES

This section provides a taster for other hand embroidery stitches not generally linked with the counted thread technique. It features some of the simplest and most popular stitches used all over the world.

History and geography have played their part in the art of embroidery. For centuries wherever people have spun cotton, linen, silk or wool, embroidery of one kind or another has flourished; and wherever they have travelled, the stitches have been copied and adapted.

The design on this page was produced as an iron-on transfer in the 1950s but it has its origins in the crewel embroidery of the English Jacobean period, which had been influenced by oriental styles and, in turn, travelled on westward to America with the early settlers.

Decorated running stitch

Even a row of plain running stitch can look interesting when laced or whipped with a second color. Secure the thread to existing stitches on the wrong side and bring the needle through.

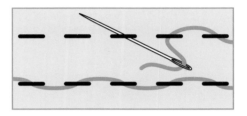

1 Lace by sliding the needle alternately up and down through the stitches without piercing the fabric until the end, when you fasten off on the wrong side.

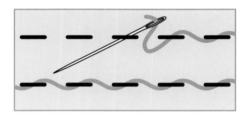

2 Whip by sliding the needle through each stitch from top to bottom only, without piercing the fabric until the end, when you fasten off on the wrong side.

Satin stitch

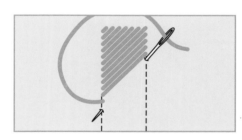

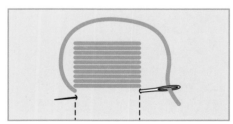

Satin stitch most probably originated in China, designed to show off the beautiful silk threads produced there. Work the stitches very closely together to cover the fabric completely. Needle in and out at the same angle and keep to a sharply defined outline.

Stem stitch

This useful stitch is a variation on the backstitch and can follow curves or straight lines.

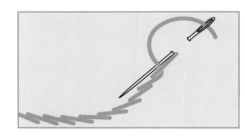

1 Work slanted backstitches with the needle coming out a little above the previous stitch.

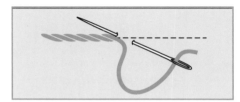

2 Create a thicker, more rope-like effect by inserting the needle at a sharper angle and increasing the number of strands to your thread.

Chain stitch

A looped stitch that is perfect for outlining and filling. It constructs well with three or more strands of embroidery cotton [floss].

 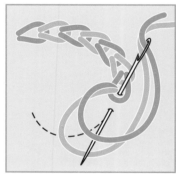

1 Bring the needle through and push in again beside the exit hole. Leave a loop on the right side and bring the needle up through it at a short distance below the starting point. Pull gently until you have formed a rounded link in the chain.

2 Thread your needle with two colors and work alternate chain stitches with them. Take care to keep the unused thread *above* the needle point.

Daisy (Lazy Daisy) stitch

A favorite stitch for depicting flowers and leaves, this variation on the chain loop can be made to form a circle of as many petals as you wish.

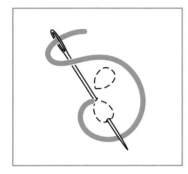 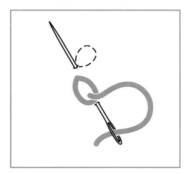

1 Begin as for chain stitch but work only one loop.

2 Instead of another link, make a very small tying stitch to hold the loop at its widest point. Bring the needle through again at the start of the next petal.

Buttonhole stitch

A relative of blanket stitch with the same basic construction. As the name suggests, this stitch evolved to seal the raw edges of a buttonhole and prevent the button rubbing the fabric. Stitched closely like satin stitch, it can be used to neaten both straight and curved edges and features in cutwork embroidery like broderie anglaise.

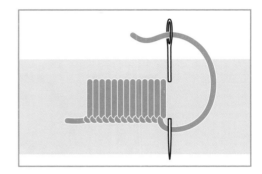

Blanket stitch

You might think this stitch belongs to domestic sewing rather than embroidery and it did indeed originate for the practical purpose of hemming blankets and towels. Today it is more likely to be used purely decoratively.

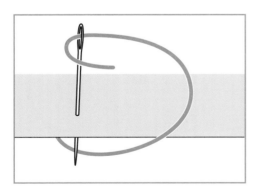  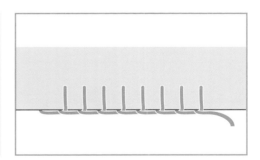

1 Secure the thread on the wrong side and bring it through at the folded edge of your fabric. Needle in at the desired stitch height and about ³/₈ in [1 cm] to the right, and out again directly below.

2 Pass the needle forward through the loop, forming a half-hitch, and tighten the thread against the fold.

3 Repeat to form a row and fasten off with an extra half-hitch around the final loop before running the end into the fabric fold.

A script alphabet imitates handwriting. This one can be used both for
cross-stitch and as an outline for free embroidery in stem or chain stitch.

WASHING, MOUNTING AND AFTERCARE

Washing embroidery

However carefully you keep your work and hands clean, there are times when a completed embroidery needs freshening up. You may have an old family heirloom that you would like to clean or a second-hand item discovered in a charity shop.

Most contemporary embroidery threads are colorfast, but older ones may not be and hand-dyed threads will certainly run. Dark colors and all shades of red are the colors to be most wary of. If you have any doubts, make a test before plunging the entire piece into the wash. You can either soak short lengths of thread in hot water for a few minutes, or press a damp cotton wool pad against the stitching (preferably on the wrong side). If it runs, or stains the cotton wool, the embroidery must be dry cleaned.

If your piece is marked with wine, ink, grease or rust, there are several proprietary stain removers you could try before laundering; always follow the manufacturer's instructions on these products.

Embroidery should be hand washed in lukewarm water only. Use pure soap flakes or a liquid detergent suitable for delicates. Remove dirt by gently pressing and squeezing; do not rub the stitching. Rinse in several changes of cool water before rolling the embroidery in a clean towel to remove excess water. Unwrap and gently pull the piece into shape.

Spread another (dry) towel over a work surface or airing rack and lay the item out flat so moisture evaporates evenly from the surface. Do not dry by direct heat or in strong sunlight.

If the piece has become distorted and will not dry square, block it by stretching and pinning on to a soft board (like foam board) using long, stainless steel pins at frequent intervals all round the edge. Leave until totally dry.

Pressing

Embroidery is always ironed *face down* on a clean padded surface, and usually with a pressing cloth between the back of the work and the iron. This prevents the stitching from being flattened and losing its texture. Check that the heat setting is correct for the fabric. If you are not using a steam iron, dampen the pressing cloth to cope with any heavy creases.

Steam treatment helps to smooth out fabric that has been worked in a hoop. Hold the iron above the embroidery, passing it to and fro until the piece is evenly damp; then pull the fabric gently into shape, eliminating the bulge made by the hoop. Lay the embroidery face down again and—without a pressing cloth, so you can see what you're doing—press by setting the iron down and lifting straight up; don't drag it across the damp fabric. Allow the embroidery to cool where it lies.

Mounting

Although you may not want to make the frame yourself, mounting your own work is easy enough. Cut a mount from thin hardboard, mounting or foam board. Conservation board is an acid-neutral alternative. Hardboard needs to be sawn and your supplier should do this. For ordinary cardboard or foam board, use a sharp craft knife (blunt blades are actually more dangerous) together with a metal straight edge and a cutting mat. Keep your fingers behind the cutting edge.

Some people like to pad their work for display. Cut the batting to the exact size of the mount board. When using hardboard, you will mount the fabric against the rough side.

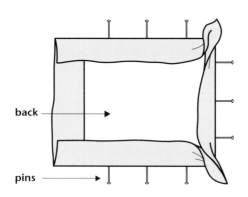

back

pins

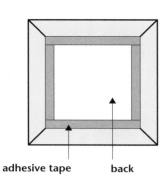

adhesive tape   back

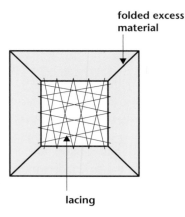

folded excess material

lacing

1 Lay the embroidery face down and place the mount board on top with the batting in between. Fold the fabric up and pin into the edges of the board using glass-headed pins. Turn and check for positioning (you may need to re-pin a few times). Ensure the edges of the board align with the weave of the fabric.

2 Hardboard will not take pins, so use adhesive tape for positioning. If you don't want any lacing, fold the corners neatly, pull the fabric taut and tape the fabric fold-over to the back of the board all round. Be aware that adhesive tape eventually turns brittle and leaves sticky deposits; it should never be used on or near the embroidered area.

3 Fold the fabric corners neatly and start lacing across the back from the middle of one of the shorter sides. Use a strong thread and work a giant herringbone stitch (p. 30) from side to side to avoid straining on a single hole in the fabric. Keep the thread tight enough to pull the surface taut without distorting the embroidery. Repeat across the two remaining sides.

Aftercare

As with every other textile, the chief enemies of embroidered fabrics are dirt, dampness and insect pests. If the piece is displayed without glass, it will need dusting. Dust builds up quickly and can absorb moisture, leading to mold. Careful use of a vacuum cleaner with adjustable suction is best. Cover the end of the cleaner hose with a nylon stocking and put the nozzle close but not touching. Fine detail can be brushed off with a clean, soft artist's brush.

If the piece is in storage, check regularly for moths. Shake it out and refold a different way; this also prevents permanent creases from setting in. Long-term storage requires that the item is put away clean, unstarched (silverfish love starch), layered and wrapped with acid-free white tissue paper. Do not store fabrics in poorly ventilated, damp or humid surroundings such as lofts, cellars and seldom-opened cupboards or chests.

TERMS AND ABBREVIATIONS

Aida Block weave fabric with regular construction and visible stitch holes

Algerian eye Cross stitch variation

Alphabets Charted letters and numerals for samplers and monograms

Anti-fray Liquid or spray to prevent fraying of cut edges

Assisi Thirteenth-century embroidery technique from the Italian town of the same name

Away waste knot Starting knot placed well away from the stitching area and later cut off

Backstitch Used to outline or define cross-stitched areas

Band Narrow strip of evenweave fabric with decorative trim

Basting Preliminary stitching, removed when work is finished

Batting [Wadding] Material used to pad mounted fabric

Binca Low-count (large scale) evenweave for use by children

Blackwork Decorative stitching, originally in black silk, brought to England from Spain in the Tudor period

Blending filament Fine metallic thread for combination with ordinary stranded floss

Blocking Stretching and pinning fabric to shape

Bodkin Large blunt-tipped needle for threading ribbon and cord

Border Decorative frame stitched around a design

Braided (woven) cross Cross stitch variation

Buttonhole stitch Neatens both straight and curved edges and features in cutwork embroidery

Chart Detailed guide to stitch placement in counted-thread embroidery, usually in the form of a grid or graph

Count Number of threads per 1 in [2.5 cm] in a foundation fabric

Counted-thread embroidery Technique of decorative stitching over a predetermined number of threads in the foundation fabric

Double cross (Smyrna) stitch Cross stitch variation

Double running (Holbein) stitch Used in blackwork and Assisi work, constructed from two passes of running stitch

Duo canvas Double thread mesh, also called Penelope

Embroidery canvas Starched woven cotton or linen mesh in four count sizes

Embroidery frame Rectangular frame to keep embroidery taut while working

Embroidery hoop Frame of concentric hoops to keep embroidery taut

Evenweave Linen or cotton fabric with the same number of identical threads per inch (2.5 cm) counted vertically and horizontally

Flower thread Unmercerized cotton twist, non-divisible, with a matt finish

Fractional stitches Quarter, half and three-quarter cross stitches

Free embroidery A form of surface embroidery not regulated by counted threads

French knot Embroidery stitch used for small details

Grid The basis of a chart or pattern, each square representing one stitch

HPI Holes Per Inch

Herringbone stitch Cross stitch variation

Holbein (Double running) stitch Used in blackwork and Assisi work, constructed from two passes of running stitch

In the hand To hold fabric in the hand while stitching, not in a hoop or frame, enabling the stitcher to sew rather than stab

Key List of symbols and associated colors on cross stitch charts

Lark's head knot (Loop start) Technique for securing thread at the start of work

Laying tool Small pointed stick of metal or wood for smoothing threads

Linen High-count woven fabric with threads of irregular thickness, made from flax

Long armed cross stitch Cross stitch variation

Loop start (Lark's head knot) Technique for securing thread at the start of work

Making up Stretching and mounting finished work

Mercerized cotton Thread treated with sodium hydroxide to strengthen, add luster and make easier to dye

Metallics Threads incorporating metal and textile fibers

Mono canvas Single thread mesh

Motif One single design element

Open filling stitch Cross stitch variation

Pearl Shiny 2-ply twisted thread, non-divisible

Perforated paper Thin card perforated with holes in a grid formation in imitation of Victorian-style stitched cards and mottos

Plastic canvas Plastic perforated to form a rigid mesh and available in pre-cut shapes

RS Right side

Railroading Technique of separating and smoothing strands of thread while stitching

Rice stitch Cross stitch variation

S-twist Threads spun counter-clockwise

Sampler Decorative means of displaying a variety of embroidery stitches

Skein Length of embroidery floss held together by paper tubes, trademarked and color coded for reference

Smyrna (double cross) stitch Cross stitch variation

Space-dyed Different colors or shades, factory dyed at regular intervals along the thread

Stab method Used with a hoop or frame: stab the needle into the fabric and pull it through from the other side

Stranded Cotton or rayon floss consisting of divisible strands

Threaded herringbone stitch Cross stitch variation

Tied cross stitch Cross stitch variation

Tweeding Different colored strands threaded into the same needle, used for textural effect

Variegated Factory-dyed single color ranging from light to dark at regular intervals along the thread

Vilene Non-woven interfacing, available plain or iron-on

Wadding [Batting] Material used to pad mounted fabric

WS Wrong side

Waste knot Starting knot placed on RS of fabric and later cut off

Woven (braided) cross Cross stitch variation

Z-twist Threads spun clockwise